TEXT
ME

1/2 cup Hugs
4 tsp Kisses
4 cups Love
1 cup Special Holiday Cheer
1/2 cup sweetheart hugs
3 tsp cinnamon hearts
2 cups Love and Kindness
1 bag of Valentines
1 medium-size bag of great big red hearts
(the regular kind won't do!)

Blend all and sprinkle with lots of love!

By organizing some

fun

Valentine's Day

celebrations,

you can lift the mood

and

spread some cheer

Many believe the X symbol became synonymous with the kiss in medieval times.

Valentine Ideas For Employees

Valentines is a great time to show appreciation in the workplace & create camaraderie between employees

Make / Decorate Cookies

Change work hours (start a hour late)

Host breakfast

Decorate the office

Hand out goody bags

Hire yoga instructor

Do game hour with prizes

In 1537,
England's
King Henry VII
officially declared
Feb. 14
the holiday of
St. Valentine's Day.

Valentines Ideas for Seniors

Valentine's Day is a great excuse to spend quality time with the senior in your life & share memories

Send flowers

Write a poem

Make a photo album

Make a goodie bag

Have a movie night

Have supper together

Send balloons

Drop off a houseplant

About 1 billion Valentine's Day cards are exchanged each year.

Valentines Ideas for Him

Homemade coupon book

Shaving kit

Homemade card

Goodie basket

Snacks (etc) subscription

Home made supper

Send him flowers !!

New plush robe / slippers

Game night

Its a special day and you want to wow the special man in your life

Richard Cadbury produced the first box of chocolates for Valentine's Day in the late 1800s.

Valentine Ideas for Her

What a great day to show her your love !

Roses are never wrong

A poem / love letter

Chocolate / Teddy Bear

Fuzzy blanket

Coupon book

Take the kids out

Candle / oil set

Romantic supper

Name a star after her (online)

Valentine's Day
is the second most
popular day of the year
for sending cards.
Christmas
is the first
most popular

Valentines ideas for your teen

Spoil

Candy box

your

Gift card for coffee shop

Heart pancakes breakfast or supper

Teen

Beauty / swag bag

Cute mug

with

Keychain

Game night they pick

LOVE

Candle making kit

New hoodie / jacket

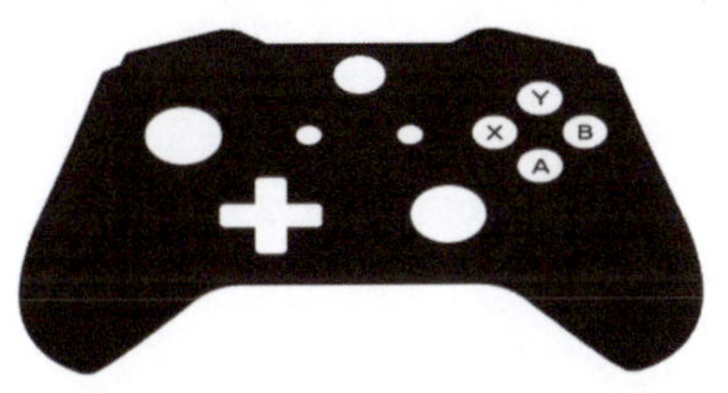

3 per cent of pet owners will give Valentine's Day gifts to their pets.

Valentine Ideas for your kids

Your little one will love their valentines !!

Valentine pajamas

Teddy Bear

New craft set / crayons / art

Valentine outfit

Chocolate (so many fun options)

Bath bomb set

Book (you read together)

Jumbo puzzle set

Baking set

Playdough (you can make your own)

I love you
What more can I say
You are my whole life
Each and every day
You are my Valentine
Today and forever more
You are the one
I will always adore

Valentine ideas for your Pets

Your furry friends need love on this special day !!

Go for a long walk

Give your pet a massage

Fun valentine treats

Dress them up

Take special pictures

Arrange a playdate

Extra snuggle time

New playtoys

DID YOU KNOW?

Valentine candy "conversation hearts" have a shelf life of five years.

Love, Love, Love
(tune: 3 Blind Mice)

Love, love, love,

love, love, love

See how it grows,

See how it grows.

I love my friends

and they love me.

We love each other

that's plain to see.

There's plenty for a

big family.

Love, love, love,

love, love, love

V

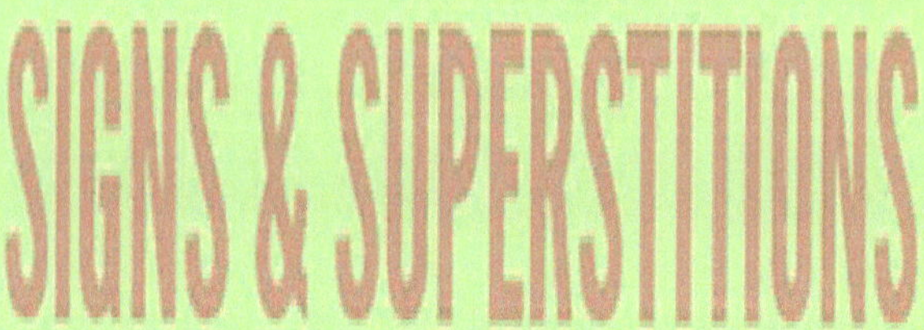

For centuries there have been signs and superstitions about love, causing plenty of enchanting ideas surrounding Valentine's Day. So, be aware of the subtle signals you give off and the ones that just happen.

VALENTINE'S DAY

EASIEST
PLAY DOUGH
RECIPE EVER

1 Cup Flour
1/ 4 Cup Salt
1/ 2 Hot Water
2 tbsp Oil
Food Colouring

STRAWBERRY ROLL-UPS

- 4 (6 inch) soft Tortialls
- Low-fat Strawberry Cream Cheese or Cottage Cheese
- 4 Tbs Strawberry Jam
- Strawberries

Spread the cheese on each tortilla.

Add 1 Tbs jam and sliced strawberries.

Fold in the edges and roll.

Slice into 2 inch bites.

Happy Valentine's Day

This coupon entitles you to one extra dessert

This coupon entitles you to an extra half hour of television

This coupon entitles you to get out of one chore

This coupon entitles you to choose a movie night

This coupon entitles you to choose dinner

This coupon entitles you to an extra bedtime story

This coupon entitles you to 1/2 an hour with Mom & Dad

Happy Valentine's Day

This coupon entitles you to
____

This coupon entitles you to
____

This coupon entitles you to
____

This coupon entitles you to
____

This coupon entitles you to
____

This coupon entitles you to
____

This coupon entitles you to
____

VOUCHER REDEEMABLE
DATE FOR
Ice-Cream

VOUCHER REDEEMABLE
DATE FOR
Movie

VOUCHER REDEEMABLE
DATE FOR
Dinner

VOUCHER REDEEMABLE
DATE FOR
Breakfast in Bed

VOUCHER REDEEMABLE
DATE FOR
Hug & Kisses

VOUCHER REDEEMABLE
DATE FOR
You Pick

VOUCHER REDEEMABLE
DATE FOR
An Adventure

VOUCHER REDEEMABLE
DATE FOR
Back Massage

you are
SO
SWEET

Happy Valentine's Day

To: _______________________

From: _______________________

Whale you be my valentine?
Happy Valentine's Day!

You're TURTLE-Y awesome!
Happy Valentine's Day!

WHAT DOES THIS FOX SAY?
HAPPY VALENTINE'S DAY!

Whale you be my valentine?
Happy Valentine's Day!

WHAT DOES THIS FOX SAY?
HAPPY
VALENTINE'S
DAY!

You're TURTLE-Y awesome!
Happy Valentine's Day!

i ♥ U
HOLD MY HAND
A sweet for my sweetie from Jenny
amy
YOU'RE HAND-SOME
I LOVE LINE!
4get me not
DAD

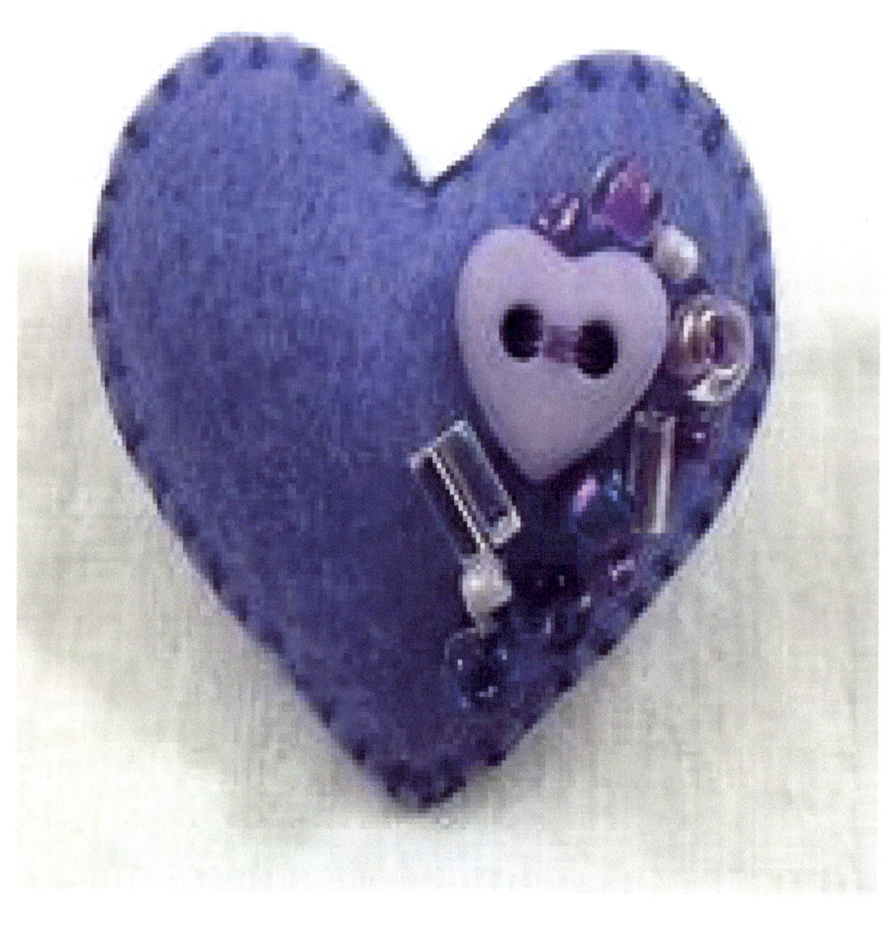

Happy Valentines

From My Family to

Yours

I
YOU